Family Tree

Name: _______________________

Date: _______________

Home Sweet Home...

| GRANDFATHER | FATHER | NIECE | SISTER | SON | DAUGHTER |
| UNCLE | BROTHER | MOTHER | AUNT | GRANDMOTHER | NEPHEW |

1. RTEAHF _ _ _ _ _ _

2. RHTEMO _ _ _ _ _ _

3. OSN _ _ _

4. RGATHDEU _ _ _ _ _ _ _ _

5. NELUC _ _ _ _ _

6. UTNA _ _ _ _

7. NHEWPE _ _ _ _ _ _

8. IECNE _ _ _ _ _

9. TSIESR _ _ _ _ _ _

10. GNRAHERFTDA _ _ _ _ _ _ _ _ _ _ _

11. DHRATNEMGRO _ _ _ _ _ _ _ _ _ _ _

12. HBRROTE _ _ _ _ _ _ _

Write MOTHER 5 times:

____

____

____

____

Family Tree

Home Sweet Home...

<table>
<tr><td>GRANDFATHER</td><td>FATHER</td><td>NIECE</td><td>SISTER</td><td>SON</td><td>DAUGHTER</td></tr>
<tr><td>UNCLE</td><td>BROTHER</td><td>MOTHER</td><td>AUNT</td><td>GRANDMOTHER</td><td>NEPHEW</td></tr>
</table>

1. RTEAHF   F A T H E R

2. RHTEMO   M O T H E R

3. OSN   S O N

4. RGATHDEU   D A U G H T E R

5. NELUC   U N C L E

6. UTNA   A U N T

7. NHEWPE   N E P H E W

8. IECNE   N I E C E

9. TSIESR   S I S T E R

10. GNRAHERFTDA   G R A N D F A T H E R

11. DHRATNEMGRO   G R A N D M O T H E R

12. HBRROTE   B R O T H E R

Write MOTHER 5 times:

[Student worksheet has a 5 line writing exercise here.]

Fruits

It is fruit time!

PAPAYA	CHERRY	STRAWBERRY	APPLE	PRUNES	FIGS
BANANA	DATE	APRICOT	AVOCADO		

1. PLPEA   _ _ _ _ _

2. PATRCOI   _ _ _ _ _ _ _

3. AAANBN   _ _ _ _ _ _

4. CDAOAOV   _ _ _ _ _ _ _

5. PAPAAY   _ _ _ _ _ _

6. TABRRERYSW   _ _ _ _ _ _ _ _ _ _

7. UEPSRN   _ _ _ _ _ _

8. ADTE   _ _ _ _

9. HECYRR   _ _ _ _ _ _

10. GIFS   _ _ _ _

Fruits

It is fruit time!

| PAPAYA | CHERRY | STRAWBERRY | APPLE | PRUNES | FIGS |
| BANANA | DATE | APRICOT | AVOCADO | | |

1. PLPEA   A P P L E

2. PATRCOI   A P R I C O T

3. AAANBN   B A N A N A

4. CDAOAOV   A V O C A D O

5. PAPAAY   P A P A Y A

6. TABRRERYSW   S T R A W B E R R Y

7. UEPSRN   P R U N E S

8. ADTE   D A T E

9. HECYRR   C H E R R Y

10. GIFS   F I G S

Hobbies

What do you like to do in your free time?

| COLORING | SEWING | READING | ACTING | BAKING | KNITTING |
| CLEANING | DRAWING | BOWLING | PAINTING | | |

1. ATCIGN   _ _ _ _ _ _

2. NGABIK   _ _ _ _ _ _

3. ONIGBLW   _ _ _ _ _ _ _

4. PNIGTAIN   _ _ _ _ _ _ _ _

5. AWDRIGN   _ _ _ _ _ _ _

6. EALCNNIG   _ _ _ _ _ _ _ _

7. SGWIEN   _ _ _ _ _ _

8. EGNDAIR   _ _ _ _ _ _ _

9. IGKNTTNI   _ _ _ _ _ _ _ _

10. OLGCNIRO   _ _ _ _ _ _ _ _

Write down your hobbies:

Hobbies

What do you like to do in your free time?

COLORING	SEWING	READING	ACTING	BAKING	KNITTING
CLEANING	DRAWING	BOWLING	PAINTING		

1. ATCIGN — A C T I N G

2. NGABIK — B A K I N G

3. ONIGBLW — B O W L I N G

4. PNIGTAIN — P A I N T I N G

5. AWDRIGN — D R A W I N G

6. EALCNNIG — C L E A N I N G

7. SGWIEN — S E W I N G

8. EGNDAIR — R E A D I N G

9. IGKNTTNI — K N I T T I N G

10. OLGCNIRO — C O L O R I N G

Write down your hobbies:

[Student worksheet has a 5 line writing exercise here.]

Jobs

What is your dream job?

ENGIENEER	SURVEYOR	ACCOUNTANT	POLICEMAN	MAID	SALESWOMAN
ELECTRICIAN	DIRECTOR	ACTOR	BANKER		

1. NERKBA   _ _ _ _ _ _

2. EREGNIENE   _ _ _ _ _ _ _ _ _

3. CNTOCAUATN   _ _ _ _ _ _ _ _ _ _

4. OMCIANLPE   _ _ _ _ _ _ _ _ _

5. OWMEASLASN   _ _ _ _ _ _ _ _ _ _

6. IDMA   _ _ _ _

7. NTIAICELCER   _ _ _ _ _ _ _ _ _ _ _

8. RYVEOSRU   _ _ _ _ _ _ _ _

9. OTRAC   _ _ _ _ _

10. OECTIDRR   _ _ _ _ _ _ _ _

Choose 5 jobs from above:

....

....

....

....

....

Jobs

What is your dream job?

ENGIENEER	SURVEYOR	ACCOUNTANT	POLICEMAN	MAID	SALESWOMAN
ELECTRICIAN	DIRECTOR	ACTOR	BANKER		

1. NERKBA   B A N K E R

2. EREGNIENE   E N G I E N E E R

3. CNTOCAUATN   A C C O U N T A N T

4. OMCIANLPE   P O L I C E M A N

5. OWMEASLASN   S A L E S W O M A N

6. IDMA   M A I D

7. NTIAICELCER   E L E C T R I C I A N

8. RYVEOSRU   S U R V E Y O R

9. OTRAC   A C T O R

10. OECTIDRR   D I R E C T O R

Choose 5 jobs from above:

[Student worksheet has a 5 line writing exercise here.]

Sports

Name: ______________________

Date: ______________

Let us have fun and be healthy!

BADMINTON	ARCHERY	AEROBATICS	GLIDING	DODGEBALL	PARACHUTING
SURFING	TENNIS	NETBALL	SEPAK TAKRAW		

1. ETCOBSIRAA   _ _ _ _ _ _ _ _ _

2. DIINLGG   _ _ _ _ _ _ _

3. NAUAIRGCTPH   _ _ _ _ _ _ _ _ _ _ _

4. CARHRYE   _ _ _ _ _ _ _

5. BAIOTNNMD   _ _ _ _ _ _ _ _ _

6. ISNTNE   _ _ _ _ _ _

7. PSEKA ARTAWK   _ _ _ _   _ _ _ _ _ _

8. ELLBNAT   _ _ _ _ _ _ _

9. UGRSNIF   _ _ _ _ _ _

10. BOAGELDDL   _ _ _ _ _ _ _ _ _

Sports

Let us have fun and be healthy!

| BADMINTON | ARCHERY | AEROBATICS | GLIDING | DODGEBALL | PARACHUTING |
| SURFING | TENNIS | NETBALL | SEPAK TAKRAW | | |

1. ETCOBSIRAA — AEROBATICS

2. DIINLGG — GLIDING

3. NAUAIRGCTPH — PARACHUTING

4. CARHRYE — ARCHERY

5. BAIOTNNMD — BADMINTON

6. ISNTNE — TENNIS

7. PSEKA ARTAWK — SEPAK TAKRAW

8. ELLBNAT — NETBALL

9. UGRSNIF — SURFING

10. BOAGELDDL — DODGEBALL

Animals #1

Let us learn about animals!

| BUFFALO | LION | JACANA | LYNX | SQUIRREL | SNAKE |
| GIRAFFE | WILD CAT | ELEPHANT | MONKEY | | |

1. KANSE _ _ _ _ _

2. OINL _ _ _ _

3. ONMYKE _ _ _ _ _ _

4. EGIRAFF _ _ _ _ _ _ _

5. ULERQSRI _ _ _ _ _ _ _ _

6. NAAJCA _ _ _ _ _ _

7. NYLX _ _ _ _

8. LUFBFOA _ _ _ _ _ _ _

9. ALNHEPET _ _ _ _ _ _ _ _

10. ILDW ATC _ _ _ _   _ _ _

Animals #1

Let us learn about animals!

| BUFFALO | LION | JACANA | LYNX | SQUIRREL | SNAKE |
| GIRAFFE | WILD CAT | ELEPHANT | MONKEY | | |

1. KANSE   S N A K E

2. OINL   L I O N

3. ONMYKE   M O N K E Y

4. EGIRAFF   G I R A F F E

5. ULERQSRI   S Q U I R R E L

6. NAAJCA   J A C A N A

7. NYLX   L Y N X

8. LUFBFOA   B U F F A L O

9. ALNHEPET   E L E P H A N T

10. ILDW ATC   W I L D   C A T

Fruits

Name: _____________________

Date: _____________

It is fruit time!

| GUAVA | PEACH | GRAPES | SOURSOP | PEAR | LEMON |
| KIWI | LONGAN | PLUM | ORANGE | | |

1. VGAUA   _ _ _ _ _

2. PRASEG   _ _ _ _ _ _

3. MONLE   _ _ _ _ _

4. IKWI   _ _ _ _

5. ALGONN   _ _ _ _ _ _

6. ENGROA   _ _ _ _ _ _

7. PAER   _ _ _ _

8. PECAH   _ _ _ _ _

9. MLPU   _ _ _ _

10. PUSOSOR   _ _ _ _ _ _ _

Fruits

It is fruit time!

| GUAVA | PEACH | GRAPES | SOURSOP | PEAR | LEMON |
| KIWI | LONGAN | PLUM | ORANGE | | |

1. VGAUA   G U A V A

2. PRASEG   G R A P E S

3. MONLE   L E M O N

4. IKWI   K I W I

5. ALGONN   L O N G A N

6. ENGROA   O R A N G E

7. PAER   P E A R

8. PECAH   P E A C H

9. MLPU   P L U M

10. PUSOSOR   S O U R S O P

Hobbies

What do you like to do in your free time?

POTTERY	WRITING	PUZZLES	ZUMBA	COLLECTING	BREADMAKING
LEGO BUILDING	COOKING	WEAVING	YOGA		

1. CGOELNILTC
    _ _ _ _ _ _ _ _ _ _

2. RBEIANMADKG
    _ _ _ _ _ _ _ _ _ _ _

3. TOYETPR
    _ _ _ _ _ _ _

4. NCOOGKI
    _ _ _ _ _ _ _

5. GNIWVAE
    _ _ _ _ _ _ _

6. EGLO IBLUDGNI
    _ _ _ _ _ _ _ _ _ _ _ _

7. ZLSEUPZ
    _ _ _ _ _ _ _

8. IGITRNW
    _ _ _ _ _ _ _

9. YOAG
    _ _ _ _

10. UBAMZ
    _ _ _ _ _

Write down your hobbies:

Hobbies

What do you like to do in your free time?

POTTERY	WRITING	PUZZLES	ZUMBA	COLLECTING	BREADMAKING
LEGO BUILDING	COOKING	WEAVING	YOGA		

1. CGOELNILTC   C O L L E C T I N G

2. RBEIANMADKG   B R E A D M A K I N G

3. TOYETPR   P O T T E R Y

4. NCOOGKI   C O O K I N G

5. GNIWVAE   W E A V I N G

6. EGLO IBLUDGNI   L E G O   B U I L D I N G

7. ZLSEUPZ   P U Z Z L E S

8. IGITRNW   W R I T I N G

9. YOAG   Y O G A

10. UBAMZ   Z U M B A

Write down your hobbies:

[Student worksheet has a 5 line writing exercise here.]

Jobs

What is your dream job?

WRITER	ARTIST	ANALYSTS	PRODUCER	DESIGNER	SINGER
EDITOR	DANCER	ATHLETE	COACH		

1. RTAIST   _ _ _ _ _ _

2. AELETHT   _ _ _ _ _ _ _

3. AYNLSSTA   _ _ _ _ _ _ _ _

4. RRTIEW   _ _ _ _ _ _

5. DRACNE   _ _ _ _ _ _

6. DEROTI   _ _ _ _ _ _

7. OAHCC   _ _ _ _ _

8. ISRDGEEN   _ _ _ _ _ _ _ _

9. OURRCPDE   _ _ _ _ _ _ _ _

10. GREISN   _ _ _ _ _ _

Choose 5 jobs from above:

Jobs

What is your dream job?

WRITER	ARTIST	ANALYSTS	PRODUCER	DESIGNER	SINGER
EDITOR	DANCER	ATHLETE	COACH		

1. RTAIST   A R T I S T

2. AELETHT   A T H L E T E

3. AYNLSSTA   A N A L Y S T S

4. RRTIEW   W R I T E R

5. DRACNE   D A N C E R

6. DEROTI   E D I T O R

7. OAHCC   C O A C H

8. ISRDGEEN   D E S I G N E R

9. OURRCPDE   P R O D U C E R

10. GREISN   S I N G E R

Choose 5 jobs from above:

[Student worksheet has a 5 line writing exercise here.]

Sports

Let us stay fit and healthy!

HIKING	KARATE	BOXING	JUDO	FRISBEE	SHOOTING
SUMO	CYCLING	FENCING	SNOOKER		

1. FSIEREB   _ _ _ _ _ _ _

2. KIGHIN   _ _ _ _ _ _

3. IGCLNYC   _ _ _ _ _ _ _

4. SOMU   _ _ _ _

5. DJUO   _ _ _ _

6. OXIBNG   _ _ _ _ _ _

7. AAKERT   _ _ _ _ _ _

8. GHOIOSTN   _ _ _ _ _ _ _ _

9. FCNGINE   _ _ _ _ _ _

10. RSKOONE   _ _ _ _ _ _ _

Write KARATE 5 times:

Sports

Let us stay fit and healthy!

HIKING	KARATE	BOXING	JUDO	FRISBEE	SHOOTING
SUMO	CYCLING	FENCING	SNOOKER		

1. FSIEREB   F R I S B E E

2. KIGHIN   H I K I N G

3. IGCLNYC   C Y C L I N G

4. SOMU   S U M O

5. DJUO   J U D O

6. OXIBNG   B O X I N G

7. AAKERT   K A R A T E

8. GHOIOSTN   S H O O T I N G

9. FCNGINE   F E N C I N G

10. RSKOONE   S N O O K E R

Write KARATE 5 times:

[Student worksheet has a 5 line writing exercise here.]

Fruits

It is fruit time!

BLACKBERRIES	DURIAN	MANGOSTEEN	BLUEBERRIES	HONEYDEW	CARAMBOLA
ACEROLA	PINEAPPLE	DRAGONFRUIT	GRAPEFRUIT		

1. OCARAEL   A _ _ _ _ _ _

2. ELIRABCBRSKE   B _ _ _ _ _ _ _ _ _ _ _

3. ISBUEBREERL   B _ _ _ _ _ _ _ _ _ _

4. ACRAMAOLB   C _ _ _ _ _ _ _ _

5. ARNIUD   D _ _ _ _ _ _

6. FPTUIREARG   G _ _ _ _ _ _ _ _ _

7. ONDHEEYW   H _ _ _ _ _ _ _

8. TMSNNGAEOE   M _ _ _ _ _ _ _ _ _

9. RNAFRIODGUT   D _ _ _ _ _ _ _ _ _ _ _

10. EPEAPILNP   P _ _ _ _ _ _ _ _

Fruits

It is fruit time!

BLACKBERRIES	DURIAN	MANGOSTEEN	BLUEBERRIES	HONEYDEW	CARAMBOLA
ACEROLA	PINEAPPLE	DRAGONFRUIT	GRAPEFRUIT		

1. OCARAEL   A C E R O L A

2. ELIRABCBRSKE   B L A C K B E R R I E S

3. ISBUEBREERL   B L U E B E R R I E S

4. ACRAMAOLB   C A R A M B O L A

5. ARNIUD   D U R I A N

6. FPTUIREARG   G R A P E F R U I T

7. ONDHEEYW   H O N E Y D E W

8. TMSNNGAEOE   M A N G O S T E E N

9. RNAFRIODGUT   D R A G O N F R U I T

10. EPEAPILNP   P I N E A P P L E

Hobbies

What do you like to do in your free time?

SAILING	KITE FLYING	PARKOUR	BONSAI	BLOGGING	DANCE
SCRAPBOOKING	KARAOKE	TRAVEL	HUNTING		

1. ANDCE _ _ _ _ _

2. OINGGGBL _ _ _ _ _ _ _

3. ABPSONOKGCRI _ _ _ _ _ _ _ _ _ _ _

4. OAKAKRE _ _ _ _ _ _ _

5. SOBANI _ _ _ _ _ _

6. UINNHTG _ _ _ _ _ _ _

7. KRAPRUO _ _ _ _ _ _ _

8. RTEVLA _ _ _ _ _ _

9. EIKT LFGINY _ _ _ _ _ _ _ _

10. AGIILNS _ _ _ _ _ _ _

Write down your hobbies:

Hobbies

What do you like to do in your free time?

| SAILING | KITE FLYING | PARKOUR | BONSAI | BLOGGING | DANCE |
| SCRAPBOOKING | KARAOKE | TRAVEL | HUNTING | | |

1. ANDCE — D A N C E

2. OINGGGBL — B L O G G I N G

3. ABPSONOKGCRI — S C R A P B O O K I N G

4. OAKAKRE — K A R A O K E

5. SOBANI — B O N S A I

6. UINNHTG — H U N T I N G

7. KRAPRUO — P A R K O U R

8. RTEVLA — T R A V E L

9. EIKT LFGINY — K I T E F L Y I N G

10. AGIILNS — S A I L I N G

Write down your hobbies:

[Student worksheet has a 5 line writing exercise here.]

Sports

Let us stay fit and healthy!

| RUGBY | HANDBALL | SOCCER | GOLF | ICE SKATING | HORSE POLO |
| CRICKET | FISHING | CROSS COUNTRY | GYMNASTICS | | |

1. SORSC URNYCTO _ _ _ _ _   _ _ _ _ _ _ _

2. REHOS LOPO _ _ _ _ _   _ _ _ _

3. SNIFIHG _ _ _ _ _ _ _

4. ECCRTKI _ _ _ _ _ _ _

5. RESCOC _ _ _ _ _ _

6. YRUGB _ _ _ _ _

7. LFOG _ _ _ _

8. SGTMINCAYS _ _ _ _ _ _ _ _ _ _

9. AHADBLNL _ _ _ _ _ _ _

10. CIE GSATINK _ _ _   _ _ _ _ _ _ _

Write GOLF 5 times:

Sports

Let us stay fit and healthy!

RUGBY	HANDBALL	SOCCER	GOLF	ICE SKATING	HORSE POLO
CRICKET	FISHING	CROSS COUNTRY	GYMNASTICS		

1. SORSC URNYCTO   C R O S S   C O U N T R Y

2. REHOS LOPO   H O R S E   P O L O

3. SNIFIHG   F I S H I N G

4. ECCRTKI   C R I C K E T

5. RESCOC   S O C C E R

6. YRUGB   R U G B Y

7. LFOG   G O L F

8. SGTMINCAYS   G Y M N A S T I C S

9. AHADBLNL   H A N D B A L L

10. CIE GSATINK   I C E   S K A T I N G

Write GOLF 5 times:

[Student worksheet has a 5 line writing exercise here.]

Animals #2

Let us learn about animals!

SEA LION	BEAVER	BABOON	WILD DOG	FOX	MARTEN
ANTELOPE	BADGER	JACKAL	ALLIGATOR		

1. LWID DGO   _ _ _ _   _ _ _

2. IRLOGALTA   _ _ _ _ _ _ _ _ _

3. ERAEBV   _ _ _ _ _ _

4. EOTENLPA   _ _ _ _ _ _ _ _

5. TAMNRE   _ _ _ _ _ _

6. OFX   _ _ _

7. JACLAK   _ _ _ _ _ _

8. AES LOIN   _ _ _   _ _ _ _

9. BARGED   _ _ _ _ _ _

10. OABBNO   _ _ _ _ _ _

Animals #2

Let us learn about animals!

SEA LION   BEAVER   BABOON   WILD DOG   FOX   MARTEN
ANTELOPE   BADGER   JACKAL   ALLIGATOR

1. LWID DGO   W I L D   D O G

2. IRLOGALTA   A L L I G A T O R

3. ERAEBV   B E A V E R

4. EOTENLPA   A N T E L O P E

5. TAMNRE   M A R T E N

6. OFX   F O X

7. JACLAK   J A C K A L

8. AES LOIN   S E A   L I O N

9. BARGED   B A D G E R

10. OABBNO   B A B O O N

Jobs

What is your dream job?

COUNSELOR	REFEREE	SUPERVISOR	MANAGER	TAX PREPARER	TREE TRIMMER
FUNDRAISER	JANITOR	LOAN OFFICER	CLERK		

1. ENGARAM
　_ _ _ _ _ _ _

2. EREREEF
　_ _ _ _ _ _ _

3. SEPRVUOSIR
　_ _ _ _ _ _ _ _ _ _

4. JTOANIR
　_ _ _ _ _ _ _

5. TEER ERTRIMM
　_ _ _ _　_ _ _ _ _ _ _

6. ISNFRARDEU
　_ _ _ _ _ _ _ _ _ _

7. ORLUEOSCN
　_ _ _ _ _ _ _ _ _

8. OLNA IFCOFER
　_ _ _ _　_ _ _ _ _ _ _

9. XAT REPERRAP
　_ _ _　_ _ _ _ _

10. ERLCK
　_ _ _ _ _

Choose 5 jobs from above:

____

____

____

____

Jobs

What is your dream job?

| COUNSELOR | REFEREE | SUPERVISOR | MANAGER | TAX PREPARER | TREE TRIMMER |
| FUNDRAISER | JANITOR | LOAN OFFICER | CLERK | | |

1. ENGARAM — MANAGER

2. EREREEF — REFEREE

3. SEPRVUOSIR — SUPERVISOR

4. JTOANIR — JANITOR

5. TEER ERTRIMM — TREE TRIMMER

6. ISNFRARDEU — FUNDRAISER

7. ORLUEOSCN — COUNSELOR

8. OLNA IFCOFER — LOAN OFFICER

9. XAT REPERRAP — TAX PREPARER

10. ERLCK — CLERK

Choose 5 jobs from above:

[Student worksheet has a 5 line writing exercise here.]

Fruits

It is fruit time!

MANGO	WATERMELON	RAMBUTAN	RAISIN	LIME	LYCHEE
PERSIMMON	POMELO	TANGERINE	POMEGRANATE		

1. EGETAMNPRAO   _ _ _ _ _ _ _ _ _ _ _

2. WEOMATNREL   _ _ _ _ _ _ _ _ _ _

3. NIGAENERT   _ _ _ _ _ _ _ _ _

4. IISNRA   _ _ _ _ _ _

5. EMIL   _ _ _ _

6. AMOGN   _ _ _ _ _

7. PIERNMSOM   _ _ _ _ _ _ _ _ _

8. CYLEHE   _ _ _ _ _ _

9. OMLEPO   _ _ _ _ _ _

10. RANUBMTA   _ _ _ _ _ _ _ _

Fruits

It is fruit time!

MANGO	WATERMELON	RAMBUTAN	RAISIN	LIME	LYCHEE
PERSIMMON	POMELO	TANGERINE	POMEGRANATE		

1. EGETAMNPRAO   POMEGRANATE

2. WEOMATNREL   WATERMELON

3. NIGAENERT   TANGERINE

4. IISNRA   RAISIN

5. EMIL   LIME

6. AMOGN   MANGO

7. PIERNMSOM   PERSIMMON

8. CYLEHE   LYCHEE

9. OMLEPO   POMELO

10. RANUBMTA   RAMBUTAN

Hobbies

Name: _______________

Date: _______________

What do you like to do in your free time?

FISHING	EATING	MEDITATION	COLLECTING	QUIDDITCH	FISHKEEPING
BILLIARDS	RESEARCH	WALKING	FRISBEE		

1. NATIEG

＿ ＿ ＿ ＿ ＿ ＿

2. IIABLDRSL

＿ ＿ ＿ ＿ ＿ ＿ ＿ ＿ ＿

3. HEIFEGSNPIK

＿ ＿ ＿ ＿ ＿ ＿ ＿ ＿ ＿ ＿ ＿

4. ESEARRHC

＿ ＿ ＿ ＿ ＿ ＿ ＿ ＿

5. TNEIIODTAM

＿ ＿ ＿ ＿ ＿ ＿ ＿ ＿ ＿ ＿

6. NGWLKAI

＿ ＿ ＿ ＿ ＿ ＿ ＿

7. FIRBEES

＿ ＿ ＿ ＿ ＿ ＿ ＿

8. DHTIQCIUD

＿ ＿ ＿ ＿ ＿ ＿ ＿ ＿ ＿

9. GSIFIHN

＿ ＿ ＿ ＿ ＿ ＿ ＿

10. NCGIOTLLCE

＿ ＿ ＿ ＿ ＿ ＿ ＿ ＿ ＿ ＿

Write down your hobbies:

....

....

....

....

....

Hobbies

What do you like to do in your free time?

FISHING	EATING	MEDITATION	COLLECTING	QUIDDITCH	FISHKEEPING
BILLIARDS	RESEARCH	WALKING	FRISBEE		

1. NATIEG   E A T I N G

2. IIABLDRSL   B I L L I A R D S

3. HEIFEGSNPIK   F I S H K E E P I N G

4. ESEARRHC   R E S E A R C H

5. TNEIIODTAM   M E D I T A T I O N

6. NGWLKAI   W A L K I N G

7. FIRBEES   F R I S B E E

8. DHTIQCIUD   Q U I D D I T C H

9. GSIFIHN   F I S H I N G

10. NCGIOTLLCE   C O L L E C T I N G

Write down your hobbies:

[Student worksheet has a 5 line writing exercise here.]

Jobs

Name: ___________________

Date: _______________

What is your dream job?

PLUMBER	PIPELAYER	SCIENTIST	ACTUARY	NETWORK ADMIN	CARPENTER
PAINTER	DEVELOPER	MATHEMATICIAN	BIOSTATISTICIAN		

1. AYCTRAU

    _ _ _ _ _ _ _

2. TIESTISCN

    _ _ _ _ _ _ _ _ _

3. TTABIITNSAIICOS

    _ _ _ _ _ _ _ _ _ _ _ _ _ _ _

4. TEAINATIACMMH

    _ _ _ _ _ _ _ _ _ _ _ _ _

5. KWNROET DNIAM

    _ _ _ _ _ _ _ _ _ _ _

6. REELPEVDO

    _ _ _ _ _ _ _ _ _

7. NEARTCRPE

    _ _ _ _ _ _ _ _ _

8. MPLEURB

    _ _ _ _ _ _ _

9. YIRAPPLEE

    _ _ _ _ _ _ _ _ _

10. NAERIPT

    _ _ _ _ _ _ _

Choose 5 jobs from above:

Jobs

What is your dream job?

> PLUMBER   PIPELAYER   SCIENTIST   ACTUARY   NETWORK ADMIN   CARPENTER
>
> PAINTER   DEVELOPER   MATHEMATICIAN   BIOSTATISTICIAN

1. AYCTRAU   A C T U A R Y

2. TIESTISCN   S C I E N T I S T

3. TTABIITNSAIICOS   B I O S T A T I S T I C I A N

4. TEAINATIACMMH   M A T H E M A T I C I A N

5. KWNROET DNIAM   N E T W O R K   A D M I N

6. REELPEVDO   D E V E L O P E R

7. NEARTCRPE   C A R P E N T E R

8. MPLEURB   P L U M B E R

9. YIRAPPLEE   P I P E L A Y E R

10. NAERIPT   P A I N T E R

Choose 5 jobs from above:

[Student worksheet has a 5 line writing exercise here.]

Jobs

What is your dream job?

FISHER	LIBRARIAN	CHEF	TAPER	BARISTA	STONEMASON
ROOFER	FARMER	TUTOR	TEACHER		

1. FOROER _ _ _ _ _ _

2. EARPT _ _ _ _ _

3. OSTSENMONA _ _ _ _ _ _ _ _ _ _

4. CHAEETR _ _ _ _ _ _ _

5. RIRLANBIA _ _ _ _ _ _ _ _ _

6. RTTUO _ _ _ _ _

7. RMREFA _ _ _ _ _ _

8. EFHRSI _ _ _ _ _ _

9. AAIBRTS _ _ _ _ _ _ _

10. FCHE _ _ _ _

Choose 5 jobs from above:

Jobs

What is your dream job?

FISHER	LIBRARIAN	CHEF	TAPER	BARISTA	STONEMASON
ROOFER	FARMER	TUTOR	TEACHER		

1. FOROER   R O O F E R

2. EARPT   T A P E R

3. OSTSENMONA   S T O N E M A S O N

4. CHAEETR   T E A C H E R

5. RIRLANBIA   L I B R A R I A N

6. RTTUO   T U T O R

7. RMREFA   F A R M E R

8. EFHRSI   F I S H E R

9. AAIBRTS   B A R I S T A

10. FCHE   C H E F

Choose 5 jobs from above:

[Student worksheet has a 5 line writing exercise here.]

Vegetable

Do not forget to eat your vegetable okay!!

| KALE | CABBAGE | PEANUTS | BOK CHOY | ASPARAGUS | BROCCOLI |
| CHICKPEAS | SPINACH | BASIL | CORIANDER | | |

1. AAGSSPUAR   _ _ _ _ _ _ _ _ _

2. EKPCHAISC   _ _ _ _ _ _ _ _ _

3. SAUPENT   _ _ _ _ _ _ _

4. GBEACAB   _ _ _ _ _ _ _

5. ICROOBLC   _ _ _ _ _ _ _ _

6. LKEA   _ _ _ _

7. KOB COYH   _ _ _   _ _ _ _

8. PASCNHI   _ _ _ _ _ _ _

9. ILBAS   _ _ _ _ _

10. ERONCIARD   _ _ _ _ _ _ _ _ _

Write your favourite vegetable here:

Vegetable

Do not forget to eat your vegetable okay!!

KALE	CABBAGE	PEANUTS	BOK CHOY	ASPARAGUS	BROCCOLI
CHICKPEAS	SPINACH	BASIL	CORIANDER		

1. AAGSSPUAR — A S P A R A G U S

2. EKPCHAISC — C H I C K P E A S

3. SAUPENT — P E A N U T S

4. GBEACAB — C A B B A G E

5. ICROOBLC — B R O C C O L I

6. LKEA — K A L E

7. KOB COYH — B O K C H O Y

8. PASCNHI — S P I N A C H

9. ILBAS — B A S I L

10. ERONCIARD — C O R I A N D E R

Write your favourite vegetable here:

[Student worksheet has a 5 line writing exercise here.]

Animals #3

Let us learn about animals!

STORK	HYENA	RHINOCEROS	MAGPIE	GRIZZLY BEAR	DEER
PEACOCK	VULTURE	COBRA	BAT		

1. ATB
_ _ _

2. EEDR
_ _ _ _

3. YZGZLRI AEBR
_ _ _ _ _ _ _   _ _ _ _

4. ULURVET
_ _ _ _ _ _ _

5. ORNHIRESCO
_ _ _ _ _ _ _ _ _ _

6. AGPIME
_ _ _ _ _ _

7. TKROS
_ _ _ _ _

8. KCOACPE
_ _ _ _ _ _ _

9. AHNEY
_ _ _ _ _

10. BOARC
_ _ _ _ _

Animals #3

Let us learn about animals!

STORK	HYENA	RHINOCEROS	MAGPIE	GRIZZLY BEAR	DEER
PEACOCK	VULTURE	COBRA	BAT		

1. ATB — B A T

2. EEDR — D E E R

3. YZGZLRI AEBR — G R I Z Z L Y   B E A R

4. ULURVET — V U L T U R E

5. ORNHIRESCO — R H I N O C E R O S

6. AGPIME — M A G P I E

7. TKROS — S T O R K

8. KCOACPE — P E A C O C K

9. AHNEY — H Y E N A

10. BOARC — C O B R A

Hobbies

What do you like to do in your free time?

PROGRAMMING	PHOTOGRAPHY	EXPERIMENTING	GAMING	MAZES	GARDENING
CAR FIXING	ORIGAMI	WAXING	CLOTHESMAKING		

1. RGAMMPONIGR
     _ _ _ _ _ _ _ _ _ _ _

2. ACR IGNFXI
     _ _ _ _ _ _ _ _

3. KMGEIANCSHTOL
     _ _ _ _ _ _ _ _ _ _ _ _ _

4. NWIXAG
     _ _ _ _ _ _

5. EAZSM
     _ _ _ _ _

6. GTPEINENMREIX
     _ _ _ _ _ _ _ _ _ _ _ _ _

7. IRMAOGI
     _ _ _ _ _ _ _

8. PPHROTYHGAO
     _ _ _ _ _ _ _ _ _ _ _

9. GDINNEGRA
     _ _ _ _ _

10. NAGGIM
     _ _ _ _ _ _

Write down your hobbies:

Hobbies

What do you like to do in your free time?

PROGRAMMING	PHOTOGRAPHY	EXPERIMENTING	GAMING	MAZES	GARDENING
CAR FIXING	ORIGAMI	WAXING	CLOTHESMAKING		

1. RGAMMPONIGR   PROGRAMMING

2. ACR IGNFXI   CAR FIXING

3. KMGEIANCSHTOL   CLOTHESMAKING

4. NWIXAG   WAXING

5. EAZSM   MAZES

6. GTPEINENMREIX   EXPERIMENTING

7. IRMAOGI   ORIGAMI

8. PPHROTYHGAO   PHOTOGRAPHY

9. GDINNEGRA   GARDENING

10. NAGGIM   GAMING

Write down your hobbies:

[Student worksheet has a 5 line writing exercise here.]

Fruits

It is fruit time!

STARFRUIT	MANDARINE	HONEYBERRY	TAMARIND	LOQUAT	JACKFRUIT
PINEAPPLE	SALAK	WHITE CURRANT	OLIVE		

1. SAALK
     _ _ _ _ _

2. AURFTRSTI
     _ _ _ _ _ _ _ _ _

3. QOTLUA
     _ _ _ _ _ _

4. YRNHOERYEB
     _ _ _ _ _ _ _ _ _ _

5. RAKTIJCFU
     _ _ _ _ _ _ _ _ _

6. INADNREAM
     _ _ _ _ _ _ _ _ _

7. LEPEPIPNA
     _ _ _ _ _ _ _ _ _

8. ATRMDNIA
     _ _ _ _ _ _ _ _

9. WIEHT RARUNCT
     _ _ _ _ _   _ _ _ _ _ _ _

10. OEVLI
     _ _ _ _ _

Fruits

It is fruit time!

| STARFRUIT | MANDARINE | HONEYBERRY | TAMARIND | LOQUAT | JACKFRUIT |
| PINEAPPLE | SALAK | WHITE CURRANT | OLIVE | | |

1. SAALK — SALAK

2. AURFTRSTI — STARFRUIT

3. QOTLUA — LOQUAT

4. YRNHOERYEB — HONEYBERRY

5. RAKTIJCFU — JACKFRUIT

6. INADNREAM — MANDARINE

7. LEPEPIPNA — PINEAPPLE

8. ATRMDNIA — TAMARIND

9. WIEHT RARUNCT — WHITE CURRANT

10. OEVLI — OLIVE

Sports

Let us stay fit and healthy!

SQUASH	POWERLIFTING	RAFTING	SWIMMING	KAYAKING	SCUBA DIVING
KART RACING	WATER POLO	CANOEING	RALLYING		

1. SQASUH

    _ _ _ _ _ _

2. ACGNEION

    _ _ _ _ _ _ _

3. GKINAAYK

    _ _ _ _ _ _ _

4. NRITGFA

    _ _ _ _ _ _

5. RAWTE OOPL

    _ _ _ _ _ _ _ _

6. WISIMNGM

    _ _ _ _ _ _ _

7. USABC IDGIVN

    _ _ _ _ _ _ _ _ _

8. INRWLEIPGTFO

    _ _ _ _ _ _ _ _ _ _ _

9. KTAR NRIAGC

    _ _ _ _ _ _ _ _

10. LLYRGAIN

    _ _ _ _ _ _ _ _

Write SQUASH 5 times:

Sports

Let us stay fit and healthy!

| SQUASH | POWERLIFTING | RAFTING | SWIMMING | KAYAKING | SCUBA DIVING |
| KART RACING | WATER POLO | CANOEING | RALLYING | | |

1. SQASUH   S Q U A S H

2. ACGNEION   C A N O E I N G

3. GKINAAYK   K A Y A K I N G

4. NRITGFA   R A F T I N G

5. RAWTE OOPL   W A T E R   P O L O

6. WISIMNGM   S W I M M I N G

7. USABC IDGIVN   S C U B A   D I V I N G

8. INRWLEIPGTFO   P O W E R L I F T I N G

9. KTAR NRIAGC   K A R T   R A C I N G

10. LLYRGAIN   R A L L Y I N G

Write SQUASH 5 times:

[Student worksheet has a 5 line writing exercise here.]

Planets

PLANETS!!

MARS	VENUS	EARTH	NEPTUNE	SATURN	URANUS
JUPITER	MERCURY				

1. YRMCREU   _ _ _ _ _ _ _

2. UVNES   _ _ _ _ _

3. ETRAH   _ _ _ _ _

4. RASM   _ _ _ _

5. IRJPUET   _ _ _ _ _ _ _

6. NUTARS   _ _ _ _ _ _

7. ARUNSU   _ _ _ _ _ _

8. ENETNPU   _ _ _ _ _ _ _

Extra Exercise! Please list down the 5 of the planets in our solar system (without looking above)

____

____

____

____

____

Planets

PLANETS!!

> MARS   VENUS   EARTH   NEPTUNE   SATURN   URANUS
> JUPITER   MERCURY

1. YRMCREU   M E R C U R Y

2. UVNES   V E N U S

3. ETRAH   E A R T H

4. RASM   M A R S

5. IRJPUET   J U P I T E R

6. NUTARS   S A T U R N

7. ARUNSU   U R A N U S

8. ENETNPU   N E P T U N E

Extra Exercise! Please list down the 5 of the planets in our solar system (without looking above)

[Student worksheet has a 5 line writing exercise here.]

Months of the year

Which month is it right now?

JANUARY	OCTOBER	SEPTEMBER	FEBRUARY	DECEMBER	JUNE
NOVEMBER	MARCH	APRIL	AUGUST	JULY	MAY

1. YAUAJRN _ _ _ _ _ _ _

2. ERAYUBFR _ _ _ _ _ _ _ _

3. RAHMC _ _ _ _ _

4. RLPIA _ _ _ _ _

5. YAM _ _ _

6. NEJU _ _ _ _

7. ULJY _ _ _ _

8. ATGUSU _ _ _ _ _ _

9. SMBETEREP _ _ _ _ _ _ _ _ _

10. TORCOBE _ _ _ _ _ _ _

11. EONVREMB _ _ _ _ _ _ _ _

12. DMBEECRE _ _ _ _ _ _ _ _

Months of the year

Which month is it right now?

JANUARY	OCTOBER	SEPTEMBER	FEBRUARY	DECEMBER	JUNE
NOVEMBER	MARCH	APRIL	AUGUST	JULY	MAY

1. YAUAJRN — J A N U A R Y

2. ERAYUBFR — F E B R U A R Y

3. RAHMC — M A R C H

4. RLPIA — A P R I L

5. YAM — M A Y

6. NEJU — J U N E

7. ULJY — J U L Y

8. ATGUSU — A U G U S T

9. SMBETEREP — S E P T E M B E R

10. TORCOBE — O C T O B E R

11. EONVREMB — N O V E M B E R

12. DMBEECRE — D E C E M B E R

Sports

Name: ___________________

Date: _______________

Let us stay fit and healthy!

MARATHON	SKIING	BOWLING	TABLE TENNIS	BASEBALL	KABADDI
RACING	SAILING	CLIMBING	FOOTBALL		

1. OOALBTFL _ _ _ _ _ _ _ _

2. LBAESALB _ _ _ _ _ _ _ _

3. OGINBLW _ _ _ _ _ _ _

4. AELTB NTENSI _ _ _ _ _ _ _ _ _

5. ANCIRG _ _ _ _ _ _

6. OANTRHAM _ _ _ _ _ _ _ _

7. NLSIGAI _ _ _ _ _ _ _

8. NGSIKI _ _ _ _ _ _

9. AADKDIB _ _ _ _

10. BIIGLMCN _ _ _ _ _ _ _ _

Write FOOTBALL 5 times:

....

....

....

....

Sports

Let us stay fit and healthy!

MARATHON	SKIING	BOWLING	TABLE TENNIS	BASEBALL	KABADDI
RACING	SAILING	CLIMBING	FOOTBALL		

1. OOALBTFL   F O O T B A L L

2. LBAESALB   B A S E B A L L

3. OGINBLW   B O W L I N G

4. AELTB NTENSI   T A B L E   T E N N I S

5. ANCIRG   R A C I N G

6. OANTRHAM   M A R A T H O N

7. NLSIGAI   S A I L I N G

8. NGSIKI   S K I I N G

9. AADKDIB   K A B A D D I

10. BIIGLMCN   C L I M B I N G

Write FOOTBALL 5 times:

[Student worksheet has a 5 line writing exercise here.]

Vegetable

Do not forget to eat your vegetable okay!!

| CELERY | LAVENDER | FRISEE | PARSLEY | LETTUCE | SOY BEANS |
| SAGE | PEAS | CAULIFLOWER | BEAN SPROUTS | | |

1. AEBN ROPUSST   _ _ _ _   _ _ _ _ _ _

2. YSO BENAS   _ _ _   _ _ _ _ _

3. EAPS   _ _ _ _

4. EWLACLUIFRO   _ _ _ _ _ _ _ _ _ _ _

5. EYECLR   _ _ _ _ _ _

6. EIRSEF   _ _ _ _ _ _

7. VEDRNELA   _ _ _ _ _ _ _ _

8. ASEG   _ _ _ _

9. ESRALPY   _ _ _ _ _

10. UELCTTE   _ _ _ _ _ _ _

Write your favourite vegetable here:

....

....

....

....

Vegetable

Do not forget to eat your vegetable okay!!

CELERY	LAVENDER	FRISEE	PARSLEY	LETTUCE	SOY BEANS
SAGE	PEAS	CAULIFLOWER	BEAN SPROUTS		

1. AEBN ROPUSST   B E A N   S P R O U T S

2. YSO BENAS   S O Y   B E A N S

3. EAPS   P E A S

4. EWLACLUIFRO   C A U L I F L O W E R

5. EYECLR   C E L E R Y

6. EIRSEF   F R I S E E

7. VEDRNELA   L A V E N D E R

8. ASEG   S A G E

9. ESRALPY   P A R S L E Y

10. UELCTTE   L E T T U C E

Write your favourite vegetable here:

[Student worksheet has a 5 line writing exercise here.]

Animals #4

Name: _______________________

Date: _______________

Let us learn about animals!

| SEAL | PYTHON | CHEETAH | RACCOON | CROCODILE | WOLF |
| CHICKEN | CHIPMUNK | OTTER | TURKEY | | |

1. ETTOR

   _ _ _ _ _

2. CDICORLEO

   _ _ _ _ _ _ _ _ _

3. PHYNOT

   _ _ _ _ _ _

4. EHHTEAC

   _ _ _ _ _ _ _

5. PMKCUNIH

   _ _ _ _ _ _ _ _

6. ANRCOCO

   _ _ _ _ _ _ _

7. OWLF

   _ _ _ _

8. SLEA

   _ _ _ _

9. RTUKEY

   _ _ _ _ _

10. NECCKHI

   _ _ _ _ _ _ _

Animals #4

Let us learn about animals!

| SEAL | PYTHON | CHEETAH | RACCOON | CROCODILE | WOLF |
| CHICKEN | CHIPMUNK | OTTER | TURKEY | | |

1. ETTOR — O T T E R

2. CDICORLEO — C R O C O D I L E

3. PHYNOT — P Y T H O N

4. EHHTEAC — C H E E T A H

5. PMKCUNIH — C H I P M U N K

6. ANRCOCO — R A C C O O N

7. OWLF — W O L F

8. SLEA — S E A L

9. RTUKEY — T U R K E Y

10. NECCKHI — C H I C K E N

Hobbies

What do you like to do in your free time?

SAND ART	SHOPPING	SHOOTING	CROSSWORD	CAMPING	CANOEING
ICE SKATING	CARVING	CHESS	LEARNING		

1. INNGLREA   _ _ _ _ _ _ _ _

2. CRIGNAV   _ _ _ _ _ _ _

3. OROSWDSCR   _ _ _ _ _ _ _ _ _

4. CIE KASNTIG   _ _ _ _ _ _ _ _ _

5. NCAIMGP   _ _ _ _ _ _ _

6. GCIOANNE   _ _ _ _ _ _ _ _

7. TSNIOOHG   _ _ _ _ _ _ _ _

8. HOSIGPNP   _ _ _ _ _ _ _ _

9. NASD RTA   _ _ _ _ _ _ _ _

10. HCSES   _ _ _ _ _

Write down your hobbies:

Hobbies

What do you like to do in your free time?

SAND ART	SHOPPING	SHOOTING	CROSSWORD	CAMPING	CANOEING
ICE SKATING	CARVING	CHESS	LEARNING		

1. INNGLREA   L E A R N I N G

2. CRIGNAV   C A R V I N G

3. OROSWDSCR   C R O S S W O R D

4. CIE KASNTIG   I C E   S K A T I N G

5. NCAIMGP   C A M P I N G

6. GCIOANNE   C A N O E I N G

7. TSNIOOHG   S H O O T I N G

8. HOSIGPNP   S H O P P I N G

9. NASD RTA   S A N D   A R T

10. HCSES   C H E S S

Write down your hobbies:

[Student worksheet has a 5 line writing exercise here.]

Jobs

Name: ___________________

Date: _______________

What is your dream job?

DENTIST	WAITER	COOK	HOUSEWIFE	GEOGRAPHER	LAWYER
ASTRONOMER	DISHWASHER	AUDIOLOGIST	CHEMIST		

1. CKOO
     _ _ _ _

2. RHSSIEWDAH
     _ _ _ _ _ _ _ _ _ _

3. AIRWET
     _ _ _ _ _ _

4. GUDASOIILTO
     _ _ _ _ _ _ _ _ _ _

5. DETTSIN
     _ _ _ _ _ _ _

6. IOHSFEUEW
     _ _ _ _ _ _ _ _ _

7. ALRYEW
     _ _ _ _ _ _

8. EMSTIHC
     _ _ _ _ _ _ _

9. MOORNRSEAT
     _ _ _ _ _ _ _ _ _ _

10. AGOGPHEERR
     _ _ _ _ _ _ _ _ _ _

Choose 5 jobs from above:

Jobs

What is your dream job?

DENTIST	WAITER	COOK	HOUSEWIFE	GEOGRAPHER	LAWYER
ASTRONOMER	DISHWASHER	AUDIOLOGIST	CHEMIST		

1. CKOO — C O O K

2. RHSSIEWDAH — D I S H W A S H E R

3. AIRWET — W A I T E R

4. GUDASOIILTO — A U D I O L O G I S T

5. DETTSIN — D E N T I S T

6. IOHSFEUEW — H O U S E W I F E

7. ALRYEW — L A W Y E R

8. EMSTIHC — C H E M I S T

9. MOORNRSEAT — A S T R O N O M E R

10. AGOGPHEERR — G E O G R A P H E R

Choose 5 jobs from above:

[Student worksheet has a 5 line writing exercise here.]

Technology

Name: _______________________

Date: _______________

WOW!! FASCINATING!

SMART HOME	FAN	PRINTER	MICROWAVE	PHONES	INTERNET
MOUSE	HEADPHONE	TABLET	LAPTOP	TELEVISION	AIR CONDITIONER

1. AOPPTL

_ _ _ _ _ _

2. ALTETB

_ _ _ _ _ _

3. DPHENEAHO

_ _ _ _ _ _ _ _ _

4. SUMOE

_ _ _ _ _

5. SEEOIILTVN

_ _ _ _ _ _ _ _ _ _

6. CEVRAOMWI

_ _ _ _ _ _ _ _ _

7. NFA

_ _ _

8. RAI ICDONRTNEOI

_ _ _   _ _ _ _ _ _ _ _ _ _

9. NPOEHS

_ _ _ _ _ _

10. EINTNTER

_ _ _ _ _ _ _ _

11. PTRENIR

_ _ _ _ _ _ _

12. MATSR EMHO

_ _ _ _ _   _ _ _ _

Technology

WOW!! FASCINATING!

SMART HOME	FAN	PRINTER	MICROWAVE	PHONES	INTERNET
MOUSE	HEADPHONE	TABLET	LAPTOP	TELEVISION	AIR CONDITIONER

1. AOPPTL — L A P T O P

2. ALTETB — T A B L E T

3. DPHENEAHO — H E A D P H O N E

4. SUMOE — M O U S E

5. SEEOIILTVN — T E L E V I S I O N

6. CEVRAOMWI — M I C R O W A V E

7. NFA — F A N

8. RAI ICDONRTNEOI — A I R   C O N D I T I O N E R

9. NPOEHS — P H O N E S

10. EINTNTER — I N T E R N E T

11. PTRENIR — P R I N T E R

12. MATSR EMHO — S M A R T   H O M E

Vegetable

Do not forget to eat your vegetable okay!!

RADISH	MUSHROOMS	OKRA	CARROT	BELL PEPPER	GARLIC
GINGER	ONION	BEETROOT	PAPRIKA		

1. ARKO   _ _ _ _

2. AGRLCI   _ _ _ _ _ _

3. NOONI   _ _ _ _ _

4. OUHMOMRSS   _ _ _ _ _ _ _ _ _

5. EBLL RPPEEP   _ _ _ _   _ _ _ _ _ _

6. AIPRKPA   _ _ _ _ _ _ _

7. ETOOEBTR   _ _ _ _ _ _ _ _

8. RACOTR   _ _ _ _ _ _

9. EGIGRN   _ _ _ _ _ _

10. HRIDSA   _ _ _ _ _ _

Write your favorite vegetable here:

Vegetable

Do not forget to eat your vegetable okay!!

| RADISH | MUSHROOMS | OKRA | CARROT | BELL PEPPER | GARLIC |
| GINGER | ONION | BEETROOT | PAPRIKA | | |

1. ARKO — O K R A

2. AGRLCI — G A R L I C

3. NOONI — O N I O N

4. OUHMOMRSS — M U S H R O O M S

5. EBLL RPPEEP — B E L L   P E P P E R

6. AIPRKPA — P A P R I K A

7. ETOOEBTR — B E E T R O O T

8. RACOTR — C A R R O T

9. EGIGRN — G I N G E R

10. HRIDSA — R A D I S H

Write your favorite vegetable here:

[Student worksheet has a 5 line writing exercise here.]

Sports

Let us stay fit and healthy!

PAINTBALL	LONG JUMP	KUNG FU	PETANQUE	SOFTBALL	WALKING
SKYDIVING	POLE VAULT	CHESS	HOCKEY		

1. NKGU UF

     _ _ _ _ _ _

2. GOLN UJMP

     _ _ _ _ _ _ _ _

3. LEOP TVULA

     _ _ _ _ _ _ _ _ _

4. KLNAIGW

     _ _ _ _ _ _ _

5. HKOEYC

     _ _ _ _ _ _

6. LTBFAOSL

     _ _ _ _ _ _ _ _

7. SNIIDYGKV

     _ _ _ _ _ _ _ _ _

8. ESHSC

     _ _ _ _ _

9. AATPLBLIN

     _ _ _ _ _ _ _ _ _

10. ENAEQPTU

     _ _ _ _ _ _ _ _

Write HOCKEY 5 times:

Sports

Let us stay fit and healthy!

PAINTBALL	LONG JUMP	KUNG FU	PETANQUE	SOFTBALL	WALKING
SKYDIVING	POLE VAULT	CHESS	HOCKEY		

1. NKGU UF — KUNG FU

2. GOLN UJMP — LONG JUMP

3. LEOP TVULA — POLE VAULT

4. KLNAIGW — WALKING

5. HKOEYC — HOCKEY

6. LTBFAOSL — SOFTBALL

7. SNIIDYGKV — SKYDIVING

8. ESHSC — CHESS

9. AATPLBLIN — PAINTBALL

10. ENAEQPTU — PETANQUE

Write HOCKEY 5 times:

[Student worksheet has a 5 line writing exercise here.]

Animals #5

Let us learn about animals!!

| DINGO | PORCUPINE | COUGAR | TURTLE | ELK | CRANE |
| COYOTE | PENGUIN | RED DEER | ZEBRA | | |

1. ABZRE

_ _ _ _ _

2. OETCYO

_ _ _ _ _ _

3. NAERC

_ _ _ _ _

4. CRAGOU

_ _ _ _ _ _

5. URNOEPICP

_ _ _ _ _ _ _ _ _

6. RDE EDRE

_ _ _   _ _ _

7. ONDGI

_ _ _ _ _

8. LETURT

_ _ _ _ _ _

9. I KF

_ _ _

10. EUPINGN

_ _ _ _ _ _ _

Animals #5

Let us learn about animals!!

| DINGO | PORCUPINE | COUGAR | TURTLE | ELK | CRANE |
| COYOTE | PENGUIN | RED DEER | ZEBRA | | |

1. ABZRE   Z E B R A

2. OETCYO   C O Y O T E

3. NAERC   C R A N E

4. CRAGOU   C O U G A R

5. URNOEPICP   P O R C U P I N E

6. RDE EDRE   R E D   D E E R

7. ONDGI   D I N G O

8. LETURT   T U R T L E

9. LKE   E L K

10. EUPINGN   P E N G U I N

[Student worksheet has a 5 line writing exercise here.]

Technology

Name: _______________________

Date: _____________

WOW!! FASCINATING!

VACUUM	SMARTWATCH	DISHWASHER	DRONE	VR GLASSES	EBOOKS
CAMERA	MONITOR	3D PRINTER	CD PLAYER	POLAROID CAMERA	GPS

1. ROIOTNM

_ _ _ _ _ _ _

2. UVUACM

_ _ _ _ _ _

3. D3 PNREITR

_ _   _ _ _ _ _ _

4. MWSHCATTRA

_ _ _ _ _ _ _ _ _ _

5. EDRON

_ _ _ _ _

6. EARACM

_ _ _ _ _ _

7. SWAHISEDRH

_ _ _ _ _ _ _ _ _

8. DC YALREP

_ _   _ _ _ _ _ _

9. RV GSSSAEL

_ _   _ _ _ _ _ _

10. EKOBOS

_ _ _ _ _ _

11. PALODORI ARCEAM

_ _ _ _ _ _ _ _   _ _ _ _ _

12. GSP

_ _ _

Technology

WOW!! FASCINATING!

VACUUM	SMARTWATCH	DISHWASHER	DRONE	VR GLASSES	EBOOKS
CAMERA	MONITOR	3D PRINTER	CD PLAYER	POLAROID CAMERA	GPS

1. ROIOTNM — MONITOR

2. UVUACM — VACUUM

3. D3 PNREITR — 3D PRINTER

4. MWSHCATTRA — SMARTWATCH

5. EDRON — DRONE

6. EARACM — CAMERA

7. SWAHISEDRH — DISHWASHER

8. DC YALREP — CD PLAYER

9. RV GSSSAEL — VR GLASSES

10. EKOBOS — EBOOKS

11. PALODORI ARCEAM — POLAROID CAMERA

12. GSP — GPS

Vegetable

Do not forget to eat your vegetable okay!!

AUBERGINE	OREGANO	TARO	ARTICHOKE	SHALLOT	BEET
SWEETCORN	POTATO	JALAPENO	LENTILS		

1. OTTPAO   _ _ _ _ _ _

2. RCEETSWNO   _ _ _ _ _ _ _ _ _

3. AOTR   _ _ _ _

4. EBTE   _ _ _ _

5. APOEJNAL   _ _ _ _ _ _ _ _

6. HATSLOL   _ _ _ _ _ _ _

7. GNOOARE   _ _ _ _ _ _ _

8. BUEGRAENI   _ _ _ _ _ _ _ _ _

9. KROHTCIEA   _ _ _ _ _ _ _ _ _

10. SETINLL   _ _ _ _ _ _ _

Write your favorite vegetable here:

....

....

....

....

Vegetable

Do not forget to eat your vegetable okay!!

| AUBERGINE | OREGANO | TARO | ARTICHOKE | SHALLOT | BEET |
| SWEETCORN | POTATO | JALAPENO | LENTILS | | |

1. OTTPAO — P O T A T O

2. RCEETSWNO — S W E E T C O R N

3. AOTR — T A R O

4. EBTE — B E E T

5. APOEJNAL — J A L A P E N O

6. HATSLOL — S H A L L O T

7. GNOOARE — O R E G A N O

8. BUEGRAENI — A U B E R G I N E

9. KROHTCIEA — A R T I C H O K E

10. SETINLL — L E N T I L S

Write your favorite vegetable here:

[Student worksheet has a 5 line writing exercise here.]

Vegetable

Do not forget to eat your vegetable okay!

DAIKON	LEEKS	TATSOI	RAPINI	PARSNIP	YAO CHOY
CORN	PUMPKIN	RADISH	WHEATGRASS		

1. ESSAWTRHGA   _ _ _ _ _ _ _ _ _ _

2. AOY YOHC   _ _ _   _ _ _ _

3. TSTAIO   _ _ _ _ _ _

4. IIANRP   _ _ _ _ _ _

5. NORC   _ _ _ _

6. DKNIAO   _ _ _ _ _ _

7. SLKEE   _ _ _ _ _

8. INSAPPR   _ _ _ _ _ _ _

9. RSAIHD   _ _ _ _ _ _

10. UKPIPNM   _ _ _ _ _ _ _

Write your favorite vegetable here:

Vegetable

Do not forget to eat your vegetable okay!

DAIKON	LEEKS	TATSOI	RAPINI	PARSNIP	YAO CHOY
CORN	PUMPKIN	RADISH	WHEATGRASS		

1. ESSAWTRHGA — WHEATGRASS

2. AOY YOHC — YAO CHOY

3. TSTAIO — TATSOI

4. IIANRP — RAPINI

5. NORC — CORN

6. DKNIAO — DAIKON

7. SLKEE — LEEKS

8. INSAPPR — PARSNIP

9. RSAIHD — RADISH

10. UKPIPNM — PUMPKIN

Write your favorite vegetable here:

[Student worksheet has a 5 line writing exercise here.]

Animals #6

Let us learn about animals!!

PELICAN	KOALA	LIZARD	CRAB	FROG	FLAMINGO
LLAMA	GOAT	IGUANA	GAZELLE		

1. FIMNLGAO   _ _ _ _ _ _ _ _

2. ILAZDR   _ _ _ _ _ _

3. ORFG   _ _ _ _

4. BCAR   _ _ _ _

5. ELLEZGA   _ _ _ _ _ _ _

6. GTAO   _ _ _ _

7. AENCPLI   _ _ _ _ _ _ _

8. KAALO   _ _ _ _ _

9. ANGUAI   _ _ _ _ _ _

10. MALLA   _ _ _ _ _

Animals #6

Let us learn about animals!!

| PELICAN | KOALA | LIZARD | CRAB | FROG | FLAMINGO |
| LLAMA | GOAT | IGUANA | GAZELLE | | |

1. FIMNLGAO   F L A M I N G O

2. ILAZDR   L I Z A R D

3. ORFG   F R O G

4. BCAR   C R A B

5. ELLEZGA   G A Z E L L E

6. GTAO   G O A T

7. AENCPLI   P E L I C A N

8. KAALO   K O A L A

9. ANGUAI   I G U A N A

10. MALLA   L L A M A

Days of the week

Do you know the days of the week?

SUNDAY	TUESDAY	THURSDAY	WEDNESDAY	SATURDAY	FRIDAY
MONDAY					

1. YADOMN   _ _ _ _ _ _

2. TDESUAY   _ _ _ _ _ _ _

3. SNADEEYDW   _ _ _ _ _ _ _ _ _

4. UTHSAYRD   _ _ _ _ _ _ _ _

5. RAFYDI   _ _ _ _ _ _

6. ATRASYDU   _ _ _ _ _ _ _ _

7. YNSAUD   _ _ _ _ _ _

Extra Exercise! Please list down the 7 days of the week (without looking above)

Days of the week

Do you know the days of the week?

SUNDAY	TUESDAY	THURSDAY	WEDNESDAY	SATURDAY	FRIDAY
MONDAY					

1. YADOMN   M O N D A Y

2. TDESUAY   T U E S D A Y

3. SNADEEYDW   W E D N E S D A Y

4. UTHSAYRD   T H U R S D A Y

5. RAFYDI   F R I D A Y

6. ATRASYDU   S A T U R D A Y

7. YNSAUD   S U N D A Y

Extra Exercise! Please list down the 7 days of the week (without looking above)

[Student worksheet has a 7 line writing exercise here.]